MAKE A DIFFERENCE: INFLUENCE THROUGH *Accountability*

MAKE A DIFFERENCE: INFLUENCE THROUGH *Accountability*

VOLUME 2 *of the* Eagle Leadership Series for Business Professionals

Dr. Larry Little

MAKE A DIFFERENCE: INFLUENCE THROUGH ACCOUNTABILITY
Volume 2 of the Eagle Leadership Series for Business Professionals

Copyright © 2012 Dr. Larry Little.

All rights reserved. No part of this book may be used or reproduced by any means, graphic, electronic, or mechanical, including photocopying, recording, taping or by any information storage retrieval system without the written permission of the author except in the case of brief quotations embodied in critical articles and reviews.

The illustrative stories in this book, although fictional, are based on years of experience in coaching and leading professionals in the workplace. The people and companies used in these stories are imagined and the scenarios have been created to illustrate real life truths and to speak to real life situations. Any resemblance to real life people or companies is purely coincidental.

iUniverse books may be ordered through booksellers or by contacting:

iUniverse
1663 Liberty Drive
Bloomington, IN 47403
www.iuniverse.com
1-800-Authors (1-800-288-4677)

Because of the dynamic nature of the Internet, any web addresses or links contained in this book may have changed since publication and may no longer be valid. The views expressed in this work are solely those of the author and do not necessarily reflect the views of the publisher, and the publisher hereby disclaims any responsibility for them.

Any people depicted in stock imagery provided by Thinkstock are models, and such images are being used for illustrative purposes only.
Certain stock imagery © Thinkstock.

ISBN: 978-1-4759-4526-3 (sc)
ISBN: 978-1-4759-4527-0 (hc)
ISBN: 978-1-4759-4528-7 (e)

Print information available on the last page.

iUniverse rev. date: 02/25/2016

Contents

Chapter 1 1
Chapter 2 Personal Accountability...................................... 7
Chapter 3 Accountability in Others.................................. 13
Chapter 4 Emotional Intelligence 27
Chapter 5 Self-Management.. 41
Chapter 6 Social Awareness... 49
Chapter 7 Relationship Management 57
Chapter 8 Influence Through Validation and
           Affirmation.. 75
Chapter 9 REAL Boundaries and Loyalty 79
Chapter 10 Applying REAL Accountability 87

Conclusion.. 93
Works Cited 99

Chapter One

Accountability. We hear the word in almost every environment that we find ourselves a part of today. While the word certainly is a common source of discussion, the definition of the word seems to vary from person to person. Does accountability refer to corporate development? Does it refer to financial success? How about personal relationships? What about personal accountability? Can we actually hold others accountable for their behavior? Is accountability a one-size-fits-all technique that ensures the success of a task?

There are numerous definitions of accountability and a variety of ways to instill accountability in yourself and others. The truth is that accountability is simply a philosophical idea or intangible thought process unless we choose to make it personal, measurable, and thus tangible. We are choosing to focus this book around REAL accountability. REAL Accountability is a tool that we have found to be effective and powerful when used by those leaders who choose to practically apply it's concepts.

Before we begin the process of diving into the REAL accountability model let's review the personality types discovered in *Make A Difference*, which is a precursor to this book. While it is not necessary to begin with *Make A Difference*, the first book in the EAGLE Leadership series, doing so will add valuable infrastructure to your leadership and relationship strategy.

We learned in *Make A Difference* that personalities are important to the success of any relationship both personally and professionally. Understanding your own personality and how to connect with and validate those with different personalities are the key concepts discovered in this book.

If you would like to discover your personality type and how we've defined the personality types of others, check out our website at **eaglecenterforleadership.com**. There you can purchase the *Make a Difference* book as well as take the personality assessment online and immediately discover your personality type. We have described the four major personality types as animals. The four animals in our personality assessments are the much-loved monkey, the leading lion, the competent camel, and the tranquil turtle.

Let's take a moment to look at a brief overview of each of the personality types.

The Much-Loved Monkey has the ability to communicate very effectively. This person is a people-person. The monkey loves to swing from tree to tree and is, therefore, very versatile and flexible in the work environment.

Relationships are extremely important, as is recognition for a job well done. The work environment must be stimulating, or the Monkey will become bored with the job. People skills, understanding, and helping others are real strengths. The Monkey can be overly sensitive to criticism and has a tendency to "monkey around" and play when consistency and concentration are needed.

The Leading Lion has the ability to "lead the pack" with great vision. This person is very task-driven and will do whatever it takes to accomplish the mission. Being in control of the work situation is very important to the lion. He or She is decisive and goal-oriented. The Lion is confident and likes to be challenged in his or her job. This person generally desires to be in leadership positions; however, the lion must learn to delegate the details of the task to others if he or she is going to be effective. Patience is not a virtue of the lion. He or she is capable of attacking others with rudeness and uncaring dominance.

The Competent Camel has the ability to stay focused and complete the task. This person is very detail-oriented. The camel works well with a prescribed set of standards and has the ability to cross the desert until the task is completed. They work well in a systematic environment and strive hard for accuracy. Always well prepared, the camel usually has not only Plan A, but Plan B and Plan C as well. They are "go-to" people who are very dependable and loyal. Camels tend to be practical and logical although they can bring mood swings to the work environment. Once a camel begins a journey, it is extremely hard for that person to change

3

directions. This leads to inflexibility in the work place. Camels can be negative and critical toward others as well as toward themselves.

 The Tranquil Turtle has the ability to be steady and secure. This person likes well-defined procedures and expectations. The turtle brings peace, consistency and follow-through to the work place. They excel in jobs with specific skills and training.

Family is extremely important to the turtle; therefore, traveling or constant change within the work place (that interferes with home life) would bring a high level of frustration. The turtle creeps along at a slow speed and can have a hard time making decisions. The higher the stress level, the slower the turtle goes. Motivation and initiative can be real challenges for the turtle.

Personalities are important as we navigate our personal and professional lives. However, we have learned that we may not give or receive accountability in a way that is consistent with our primary personality trait. For instance someone who has a lion personality trait may actually give and receive accountability more like a monkey. Research has shown us that we receive our personalities from three basic ingredients. One is the genetics with which we were born. Our neurological makeup may actually predisposition us towards a certain temperament. Two, our environment many times drives our behavior. For instance, if you were exposed to an abusive home as a child it could skew your thought process and behavior and thus your personality. Conversely, if you were exposed to a healthy loving home, it may positively affect your behavior. Perhaps the most important piece of our personality make up is the third ingredient, which is choice. We ultimately get to choose how we respond to our genetic makeup and our environment.

Accountability is gained primarily from our environment and experience. Therefore we may actually give and receive accountability very differently than our personality makeup. That's why we created the REAL accountability model. We have divided accountability into four basic styles.

R The Relate Accountability style centers on verbal communication and relationships. This type of accountability is generally given from those who have strong people skills as well as strong verbal communication skills.

E The Execute accountability style centers on the completion of the task. This type of accountability is generally given from those who have a strong desire and ability to accomplish established goals.

A The Analyze Accountability style centers on precise measurement and process. This type of accountability is generally given from those who have a strong ability to structure and provide a keen eye for detail.

L The Listen Accountability style centers around one on one interpersonal relationship building. This type of accountability is generally given from those who have a strong ability to build consensus through mutual respect and authentic relationships.

We have developed a tool to help you assess your personal accountability style. This would be a great time to press pause and visit our website at **eaglecenterforleadership.com** to find out how you can take the REAL Accountability assessment.

Chapter Two
Personal Accountability

Accountability is about personal growth and achieving one's ultimate potential. Regardless of our aspirations in life accountability is key to being successful. It is important to be accountable to the people in our lives, obligations we make, dreams and goals we have set, challenges we have accepted, and the standards we set for ourselves.

This leads us to the question: How do you define accountability? Why is accountability important? How do we build accountability within ourselves?

I could quote Webster's definition of accountability in this space but all that we would have is an academic rendering of a philosophical idea. Defining accountability is difficult. The definition of accountability has a vast depth of scope. We all have our own perceptions and expectations around being held accountable. That is why it is vital to fully understand our own personal accountability style. Once we develop a sense of self-awareness, we will be poised to lead ourselves toward applying REAL accountability.

This begins with an understanding of how we perceive ourselves. Let's take a deeper dive into accountability on a personal level.

Relate: Overview

Those who demonstrate strong people skills influence the person who operates out of the Relate accountability type. He or she is most likely to respond to verbal expectations and affirmation. Likewise, the Relate type is generally talkative and likes to give commentary on his or her progress. He or she is motivated by accountability that is social in nature and includes public feedback when appropriate.

Relate types see accountability as something that is very personable. They buy into the old adage "relationship over rules". The Relater will generally find a way to prioritize people over the process. This may look like having an encouraging conversation or having a hard conversation with someone. The accountability will most likely be a face-to-face encounter or a group meeting. This person sees accountability as something that can be encouraging, helpful and positive. The Relater actually sees accountability as something to celebrate! The Relate accountability type believes that the best way to achieve solid, effective and powerful accountability is to influence others through a relationship.

Execute: Overview

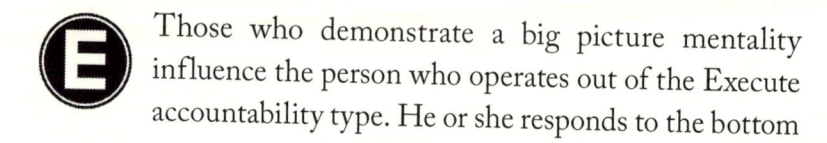

Those who demonstrate a big picture mentality influence the person who operates out of the Execute accountability type. He or she responds to the bottom line expectations that lead to completing the task; likewise, the Execute type is generally driven and likes to have a lot of freedom to operate. He or she is motivated by an accountability style that is project oriented and includes feedback once the task is complete.

The Execute type sees accountability as something that is very goal driven. This person gives and receives accountability from 30,000 feet. He or she is most effective when given large tasks to accomplish with accountability checkpoints at the completion of major landmarks that occur within the given project. Likewise this person gives accountability based on large chunks of work being accomplished. The Execute type is most comfortable looking at a large body of work rather than providing accountability for every small task along the way. He or she enjoys large challenges and thrives on competition. This person sees accountability as something that is task driven with little time for celebration. The Execute accountability type believes that the most effective way to influence others through accountability is to simply "Get the job done"!

Analyze: Overview

Those who demonstrate an ability to pay attention to detail will influence the person who operates out of the analyze accountability type. He or she responds to a laid out plan that gives the specific expectations and desired outcomes. The Analyzer needs black and white clarity. He or she is motivated by accountability that is calculated and predictable.

The Analyze type sees accountability as a process that is specific and well defined. The person will provide regular feedback when giving accountability and thrives with receiving feedback that is detailed. The Analyzer is comfortable with small tasks that lead to the bigger picture. He or she will dive into the depth of the project and find value in bringing organization to each step along the way. Creating that organization and structure provides energy and security to the Analyzer. This person can focus on a micro level to ensure the quality and success of a project. The Analyze accountability type believes that the most effective way to influence others through accountability is to provide a process that is driven by attention to detail.

LISTEN: OVERVIEW

Those who demonstrate the skill of perception influence the person who operates out of the Listen accountability type. He or she responds to well rounded and thought through expectations. Likewise, the Listen type is generally laid-back and likes to have time to meet expectations. He or she is motivated by accountability that is less structured and includes set benchmarks for feedback.

The Listen type sees accountability as being person oriented. This person gives and receives accountability when it is centered on one-on-one interpersonal relationships. Here she is most effective when given expectations that can be communicated in a private or nonthreatening manner. Consequently, this person gives accountability by authentically connecting with those he or she leads. They prefer an organization that is not overly structured and that provides for ongoing and regular feedback. In addition, the one who uses the Listen style of accountability believes that the most effective way to influence others is to provide for flexibility and change along the way toward achieving a set task or goal.

CHAPTER THREE
ACCOUNTABILITY IN OTHERS

Once we have gained an awareness of how we perceive accountability and others, it is important to develop an awareness of how others perceive accountability. Accountability to one person may look like excessive use of control to another. One person's method of influencing through accountability may appear to be a compromise to someone else. Remember, while we may not agree with another person's perception, developing awareness and understanding will allow us to successfully influence and lead in a diverse environment. It is important to recognize that in many cases perception is reality. In other words, what we say or think we see we generally treat as reality. Therefore our interpretation or misinterpretation can lead to communication issues that stifle accountability growth and relationships.

A lack of accountability can have a tragic impact on both personal and professional relationships. Unmet expectations breed frustration and disappointment with those that we have interactions. We all have experienced the disappointment of being let down by someone we thought we could trust. It is for that reason that many people choose to depend only upon themselves and refuse to trust others. We see this mindset prevalent in business environments as well as personal relationships. While this independent behavior looks good on the surface, it severely limits our ability to lead and influence others.

It is true that being independent and self-sufficient is necessary at times. However, we live in a world centered on relationships. All successful organizations, businesses, families and friendships must have effective relationships at their core.

Effective relationships can best occur when we influence one another through accountability. This is the cornerstone for successful personal and professional interactions. The good news is that being accountable to another or successfully depending on others, as well as having them depend on us is a discipline that can be learned. The process of influencing through accountability will allow us to build trust and confidence in our professional teams as well as our personal relationships.

In any successful company or organization there are stories of great abilities and successes and, in the same groups of people, stories of weaknesses and failures. Yet, those who sustain effectiveness and success are those who discover how to become accountable to one another on a daily basis. It is a process that takes work and intentionality, but the reward is well worth the effort.

With that thought in mind, let's examine how each accountability type may perceive the other three accountability styles. Later we will learn why it is important to gain an awareness of others perceptions so that we might lead and influence effectively.

RELATE: PERCEPTION OF OTHERS

The Relate accountability type may see the Execute accountability type as being over-controlling, too demanding, and excessively driven. His perception of the Execute type could be that the person is rude, abrupt, or even arrogant. This causes a negative defensive response from the Relate accountability type. It may look like the Relater seeking to avoid the Execute accountability type or possibly becoming overly emotional when leading this person. The result is that frustration arises between both parties and thus the Relater is not able to influence or lead effectively.

A possible scenario would look like this. The Relater is leading the team and arrives late to the very first team meeting. This frustrates the Execute type who is on the team and she "calls out" the Relater for being late in front of the whole group. This greatly embarrasses the Relater leading him to do one of two things at that point. One he continues the project and avoids engaging or isolates the Execute, who he considered to be an aggressive and uncooperative teammate. Two, he emotionally confronts the Execute type and determines that she is not a team player and thus invalidates her throughout the rest of the project.

Both of the responses are unhealthy, and cause miscommunication and trust on the team and in the relationship.

Relate accountability type may see the Analyze type as inhibitive, overly critical, and legalistic. Her perception of the Analyze type could be that he is more concerned with criticizing others then solving the problem. This causes the Relater to make assumptions that may lead to a lack of understanding thus causing conflict within a relationship. Since Relaters tend to be centered on people and Analyzers tend to be centered on the quality of the work, goals and objectives can easily be misaligned. From the Relater's point of view, the Analyzer may be focusing on rules instead of engaging in interacting with people.

A possible scenario may look like this. The Relater schedules a meeting with an Analyzer who is on her team. As the meeting begins the Relater shares a funny story that happened to her a couple of days ago. The story is a bit lengthy and the Analyzer realizes that they have a lot to cover and is anxious to get on with the task at hand. At the end of the story the Relater realizes that the Analyzer is not laughing or sharing in her humor. This gets the meeting off to an icy start and it never recovers. The Relater walks away from the meeting knowing that she only wants to interact with the Analyzer when she has no other choice. She views the Analyzer as negative, critical, and no fun to be around. This results in a lack of communication, and overall low team morale.

Relaters may see the Listen accountability type as diminished in their ability to communicate, hard to read, and lacking in enthusiasm. This causes the Relater to perceive that the Listener is not engaged and does not desire to be a part of a team or a relationship. The Relater perceives when people are engaged and involved in the conversation or meeting by watching their facial expressions, body language, and verbal interactions. This method does not work with Listeners. Therefore the Relater often makes assumptions that the Listener is not connected to the conversation because of the Listener's flat affect or facial expressions, laid-back demeanor, and introverted communication.

A possible scenario could look like this. The Relater is conducting a team meeting and requests feedback from the group. He notices that while most of the team members are engaged, the Listener is not offering verbal comments and seems to be disengaged. This causes the Relater leader to assume that the Listener is apathetic and unconcerned. Therefore the Relater chooses to navigate around the listener. He moves forward with the task at hand collaborating with other members of the team and making significant decisions without ever hearing the Listener's input. This causes the Relater and the team to isolate the Listener team member. The consequence is a loss of valuable information that the Listener possessed but never shared.

EXECUTE: PERCEPTION OF OTHERS

The Execute accountability type may see the Relate accountability type as being too soft, avoiding hard conversations, and only concerned with making everyone happy. This causes the Execute type to perceive that the Relater is silly, overly friendly, and attention seeking. Because the Execute type is only concerned with getting the job done she will be highly frustrated with the Relater's need for conversation, humor and engagement. Many times the result is that the Execute accountability type becomes more assertive and less tolerant of the Relater accountability type. From the Execute's perspective the Relater is wasting her time and creating an obstacle to accomplishing the task.

A possible scenario would look like this. The Execute is focused on a large project and has called a meeting to discuss strategy and implementation. She recognizes the importance of this project and approaches a meeting with intensity and determination. As she is conducting the meeting she notices that the Relater is talking to the person next to him. The last straw occurs when the Relater begins giggling in the middle of her very important meeting. This causes the Execute personality type to become even more intense and to demand that everyone on the team recognize the importance and seriousness of the job at hand. Her demeanor causes the Relater to shut down. She continues to drive the meeting but loses any authentic response from the Relater.

The Execute accountability type may see the Analyze accountability type as being too concerned with details, stifling vision, and being over-structured. From the Execute's perspective the Analyze type gets caught up in the weeds, cannot see the big picture, and allows small details to stop progress from being made. This causes the execute type to invalidate the process that is vitally important to the Analyzer accountability type. In fact, Execute accountability type will become more frustrated and more intense as he assumes that the Analyzer will constantly slow him down.

A possible scenario would look like this. The Execute type is on task to complete a huge project that he has been leading for some time. He realizes that there are some loose ends that need to be tied up in order to complete the project. As he addresses his coworker who is an Analyze accountability type, he realizes that she is going to hold his "feet to the fire" for every detail within the completion process. This perception causes him to address his coworker with direct, demanding, and even rude conversation. He thinks his best strategy is to dominate the conversation in order to move things along. However, the more intense he becomes the slower the coworker responds to what he needs. He realizes that he has no concern for her process or her attention to detail. This causes the professional relationship to strain and greatly slows down the completion of the project.

The Executor accountability type may see the Listen accountability type as slow to move forward, too pliable, and always over processing. Because the Execute type generally operates at a fast pace, she can easily run past the Listener's input and engagement in a relationship or team. Because the Listener is not likely to be aggressive or even assertive, the Execute may never recognize the value that the Listener can bring to the table. The perception of the Execute type is that since the Listener does not confront her then she will not acknowledge his connection to the team or project. The result is a loss of valuable input and a degenerated morale by the Listeners on her team.

A possible scenario would look like this. The Execute leader realizes that things are not going well on the team. She knows that there is a constant lack of communication and her divisions are polarized and thus not working together. Consequently, she calls a meeting to discuss the problem. Actually, she already knows what she is planning to do but wants to hear from her team. Each member offers ideas and suggestions; even the Listener's are trying to contribute. However, when the Listener type offers a thought or suggestion, she quickly dismisses their ideas as being too passive and soft. The result is that the Executer's team is on a self-destructive path that will negatively impact her leadership.

ANALYZE: PERCEPTION OF OTHERS

The Analyze accountability type may see the Relate accountability type, as having too little structure, not focused enough to follow through and overly spontaneous. Therefore, the Analyzer may tend to discredit or invalidate the value the Relater brings to the team or relationship. Because the Analyzer is data driven and lives in a black and white world, he can easily become frustrated with the Relater who lives in a grey, people oriented world. The perception of the Analyzer is that many times the Relater "shoots from the hip" and does not think through the long lasting consequences of his decision.

A possible scenario would look like this. The Analyzer has scheduled a phone meeting with a Relater that she leads from a remote location. As the meeting begins the Analyzer realizes that the Relater did not send the e-mail containing the data reports that were needed for the meeting. She asked the Relater about the data and he assures her that the information is "on the way". The Relater shares with the Analyzer that he has made several good connections and contacts that will greatly enhance the prospects and success of the business. She replies with, "So what can you show me with hard data to validate your efforts?" When the Relater says that he has no hard data but feels sure that his connections will lead to increased business revenue, the Analyzer feels that the Relater is once again refusing to follow through with appropriate data details. This causes the business relationships to suffer and the project to stagnate.

The Analyze accountability type may see the Execute accountability type as paying no attention to detail, having unrealistic expectations, and being too quick to take action. Because the process is vitally important to the Analyzer, the action oriented Execute type may prove to be difficult for him to lead. While the Analyzer realizes the importance of following the standard procedure, the Execute type is more concerned with getting the job done. The big picture behavior of the Executor may cause the Analyzer to become even more detailed and procedure driven. The perception of the Analyzer is that the Execute accountability type is too action oriented and will most likely overlook important details within the project or relationship.

A possible scenario would look like this. The Analyzer has been working on a business model for the upcoming project that has been assigned to him. After weeks of preparation he is rolling out his plan to his peers on the leadership team within this division. Immediately, the Execute accountability type on the team begins to look impatient and frustrated. She challenges the Analyzer by telling him that his business model is too concerned with "the weeds" and does not focus on the overall big picture of the project. She challenges his model and confronts his overall competency. At this point, the Analyzer becomes educated and realizes that he cannot work with someone who has such unrealistic expectations and impatience. While collaboration on the leadership team is essential for this project to be successful, there is a large gap between the Analyzers approach and on what the Execute accountability type is focused. This causes dissension on the team, lack of trust and ultimately poor performance.

The Analyze accountability type may see the Listen accountability type as overly concerned with personal feelings, too willing to bend the rules, and unwilling to work within set parameters. The Analyzer is task driven. When a task is presented, she believes that the process is to be followed until the task is completed. This poses a problem when leading a Listen accountability type, as the Listener needs one on one interpersonal relationships. While the Listener excels with flexible timelines and goals, the Analyzer needs much more of a solid and defined set of expectations. The laid-back and thoughtful behavior of the Listener accountability type may cause the Analyzer to react with rigid and concrete expectations. The perception of the Analyzer is that the Listener will not follow the rules and will create his own timeline to accomplish tasks, regardless of others needs.

A possible scenario would look like this. The Analyze accountability type supervisor sets expectations for the Listener team member. The expectations were precise with a high level of detail and a solid time line. The Analyzer becomes frustrated when the Listener team member does not meet the specific timelines given around the expectations. However, the Listener has assessed the situation and believes that he can accomplish the goals on a new timeline that he has set for himself. He believes that the Analyzers expectations and timelines are unrealistic and unnecessary. The Listener realizes that with his schedule he will meet the expectations of the Analyzer and he feels that the Analyzer is simply putting obstacles in his way instead of providing strong leadership and removing the obstacles that will hinder his progress. The result is a frustrated relationship between the Analyzer and the Listener. The Listener feels he is being micromanaged and the Analyzer feels that she cannot trust the Listener to complete the task in the precise manner in which she has set forth. The result is an unhealthy work relationship leading to low productivity.

LISTEN: PERCEPTION OF OTHERS

The Listen accountability type may see the Relate accountability type as overly emotional, too chaotic, and not authentic. The Listener may interpret the histrionic Relate accountability type as being unstable or unreliable to deal with difficult situations. This will cause the Listener to invalidate the ideas or suggestions of the Relate accountability type. The more excited or talkative the Relate individual becomes, the more distant and introverted the Listener becomes. In other words, the more energy the Relater brings to the relationship, the less engagement the Listener demonstrates. The perception of the Listener is that the Relate accountability type generally does not take the time to discover deep authentic relationships either professionally or personally.

A possible scenario would look like this. The Listener leader has an important topic to discuss. It is a serious matter with significant implications for the entire organization. As he attempts to discuss this with the Relater, the Listener realizes that the Relater is unfocused and does not appreciate the severity of the situation. The Listener leader then decides not to discuss the matter with the Relater. The Relater however, thinks that she is engaged and while she may appear unfocused, is actually multitasking several scenarios in her mind. The result is that the Relater feels misunderstood and the Listener feels disrespected. Consequently, the organization loses the benefit of effective problem solving from all members of the leadership team.

The Listen accountability type may see the Execute type as being too aggressive, inconsiderate of personal ramifications and coming across as dictatorial. The Listener will avoid the aggressive nature of the Execute accountability type by disengaging or by isolating the Execute type. This will cause the Execute type to become frustrated and more aggressive. As the assertive behavior of the Execute increases, the Listener leader will become more distant, polarized, and withdrawn. The Listen accountability type is defined as being introverted and person oriented. Meanwhile, the Execute accountability type is generally extroverted and task driven. This opposite disposition can cause misunderstanding and miscommunication on both a personal and professional level. The perception of the Listener is that the Execute accountability type is quick to act and slow to consider the ramifications of the action.

A possible scenario would look like this. The Listener leader is conducting a meeting with his leadership team. He is discussing a financial matter that is both important and sensitive. It is obvious that the Execute accountability type thinks she has the answer to the issue at hand. She begins to lecture the group and, in the opinion of the Listener, takes over the meeting. Seeing the frustration of the rest of the team members, the Listener leader adjourns the meeting. He subsequently calls the Executor accountability type into his office and tries to make her aware of what just occurred in the meeting. The Execute accountability type becomes agitated and begins raising her voice at the Listener leader. The Listener tells the Execute, "This meeting is over!" and asks her to leave his office. The result is a fractured relationship on a professional and personal level that negatively affects the team and the organization.

The Listen accountability type may see the Analyze accountability type as being too concerned with the process, inflexible, and micromanaging. The Listener leader believes that relationships are essential to the success of any organization and to the success of accomplishing most given tasks. The black-and-white approach of the Analyze accountability type may cause the Listener to become frustrated with the rigid process and behavior of the Analyzer. While the Listener believes that the ability to navigate is founded in the ability to be flexible, the Analyzer believes that "rules are made to be followed". The Listener may become frustrated with what she sees as the Analyzer's unnecessary need for precise detail. The perception of the Listen accountability type is that the Analyze accountability stops progress by micromanaging and thus over controlling a project or task.

A possible scenario would look like this. The Listen accountability type serves on a Leadership team with an

Analyze accountability type. The team is facing an important dilemma. Once the problem has been thoroughly explained by the leader of the team, the Listener accountability type asks for some time to think about the problem and develop a workable solution. The Analyzer realizes that there is a timeline to meet, thus there is no time to think through solutions. He suggests they follow a prescribed procedure to the letter even at the expense of the team and organization. While the Listener realizes that taking the time to think through the solution may cause them to have to push back the time line of delivery, she believes it is worth the effort. The disagreement divides the team and hinders their ability to develop workable solution to the dilemma. Therefore, the team and the organization suffer.

I realize that these perspectives were negative in nature. However, our view of others many times determines our ability to successfully influence through accountability. Influencing through accountability is a process and it begins with us becoming aware of our own accountability style. Realizing how we perceive other accountability types comes next. Understanding how others view our accountability type allows us to truly begin the journey of influencing others.

Once we have gained an understanding of accountability types the question becomes: "So what do I do with this information?"

In the next few chapters we will explore practical and effective tools that will be of much value in your quest for REAL accountability.

CHAPTER FOUR
EMOTIONAL INTELLIGENCE

If accountability centers around the awareness of yourself and others, it is no wonder that emotional intelligence has become the predominant criteria for measuring the success and failure of a professional or personal relationship.

The Harvard Review reports that EQ – short for Emotional Intelligence – is critical for managers and employees. "EQ accounts for anywhere from 24% to 69% of performance success… Some positions require more emotional intelligence than others, but there are very few jobs in which a solid level of EQ does not confer advantage. For managers it is crucial, as it is for anyone who needs to be adept at the give-and-take of working as part of a creative, dynamic team." (*Hiring for Emotional Intelligence*, Christina Bielaszka-DuVernay, November 19, 2008)

Further studies indicate that executives are interviewing and testing for EQ as well as IQ. It is important to realize that EQ is not related or contingent on IQ. In other words, you do not have to have a high EQ to achieve a high IQ. In fact, we have found that in many cases there is an inverse correlation between EQ and IQ. Consequently, a highly technically minded employee may actually have very low EQ. Likewise; an entry-level employee who does not possess the technical skills of her peers may actually possess a high EQ. Interestingly, studies have found that top performers on all levels who are successful across a sustained time are those who possess both IQ and EQ.

In today's globally driven business market, it is essential that leaders, managers, and employees understand the concept of EQ if they're going to be successful. No longer are the days when a business or corporation can thrive without building strategic relationships on the local, domestic, or international level. Healthy relationships on the professional and personal level are the cornerstone of emotional intelligence.

In *LEADERSHIP 2.0*, by Travis Bradberry and Jean Greaves, EQ is defined as "a set of skills that captures our awareness of our own emotions and the emotions of others, and how we apply this awareness to manage ourselves effectively and form quality relationships."

Bradberry continues, "Your emotional intelligence is the foundation for a host of critical skills—it impacts most everything you say and do each day. Emotional intelligence is the single biggest predictor of performance in the workplace and the strongest driver of leadership and personal excellence."

While there are numerous studies, articles and opinions around how to define and regulate EQ, we will use Bradberry's structure for understanding EQ. There are four basic components that make up someone's emotional intelligence. They are self-awareness, self-management, social awareness, and relationship management. We will take a deeper look at each component and provide tools for effectively applying each component to your relationships.

Self-Awareness

Self-awareness is the ability to accurately perceive your emotions in the moment and understand your tendencies across situations. In other words, it is becoming aware of how you are feeling in the moment. We find that many times people have a tendency to download one emotion over and over again. For example, if Fred is actually feeling fear he may download anger. Or if Angie is feeling discouraged she may act on that feeling by becoming overly critical of others.

Our brain has the capacity to experience an incredibly fast and diverse array of feelings and emotions. However, many times we suppress or hide these emotions not only from others but from ourselves as well. It is important to realize that neurologically, our brain contains a component called the Amygdala, which controls our emotional makeup. Our brain also consists of the executive functioning area, which is found in the frontal cortex area.

We will talk more about these two areas of the brain later in the book, however for now it is important to realize that emotional intelligence begins with becoming self aware of the emotional component of our brain.

In order to obtain self-awareness, we must choose to take the time to develop an intrinsic understanding of what is going on inside of us. This is a core principle of EQ. Self-awareness is a process that can be learned if we choose to self assess and allow ourselves to be honest and vulnerable with what we are thinking and feeling.

While this may sound easy, it takes practice, learning the process and developing the self-confidence to be authentic. We must be aware of our internal responses to the environment in which we find ourselves. We also must become aware and recognize triggers that cause certain emotional responses within our subconscious and within our conscience. For instance, if I grew up in an abusive violent home where my parents constantly were screaming at each other and at me, I would probably develop a trigger for raised voices. Therefore, when having conversations with others I must become aware that if a disagreement occurs and the other party begins to raise his or her voice, I may be triggered to respond emotionally. That could look like me responding aggressively or it could look like me shutting down.

Recognizing triggers within a personal or professional relationship could be the single most important factor to sustaining a successful relationship with others. Becoming aware of how those triggers make me feel is critical to successfully navigating relationships.

Finally, we must understand the predispositions that could lead to triggers. For example, if I am aware that excessive alcohol leads me to act in a violent manner, I must then ask myself the following questions: Where do I usually over drink? When do

I drink excessively and with whom do I usually consume too much alcohol?

Once I have discovered these predispositions then I can take precautions to avoid excessive use of alcohol.

Accountability begins and ends with the decision to lead oneself well. In order to lead ourselves effectively, we must choose to become self-aware. The truth is, no matter what position you hold within an organization you are influencing others. Every day, you influence those that surround you personally and professionally. Let's take a moment to discover the self-awareness tool we call the Leadership Ladder. We believe that everyone is a leader. While you may not lead others, you certainly lead yourself. The only question is are you leaving yourself well or poorly. In order to determine how well you are leading, you must take the time to become self aware of where you are on the Leadership Ladder.

Title Leadership

The first and lowest rung on the ladder is called the Title rung. Those who are on this level of the leadership ladder are simply leading from a positional standpoint. This occurs when a professional or personal relationship first begins. People recognize you because of your position or title, however no authenticity or vulnerability has occurred on any level. Your influence is limited to the policies and procedure that is tied to the position or title that you hold. There is no respect given here, only possible fear of the position that is held.

One of my favorite series is a vintage TV show called *The Andy Griffith Show*. This old comedy contains nuggets of wisdom that are still relevant to our lives today. The show centers on the sheriff, Andy Griffith, who leads a small-town with his wit and wisdom and charm. His sidekick deputy is Barney Fife. Barney is a small man with a large ego. He loves the idea of having a badge and a uniform. Many of the episodes are based on Barney's quest for respect, due to his position as "Deputy Fife". One of my favorite scenes depicts Andy having a conversation with a dejected Barney. Andy says, "Barney, people do not respect me because I wear a badge or a uniform, people believe in me because of the man behind the badge". In other words, "I don't lead from a title or position, I lead through relationships." This is a prime example of possessing EQ.

While we all must enter our relationships on this level; staying or leading for a long period of time from this rung on the ladder will cause frustration and stagnation for others and ourselves.

Team Leadership

The next rung on the ladder is Team leadership. At this stage, relationships are established. The leader begins to connect with others on a personal and professional level. Influence is gained through these connections. People align and follow you because they have developed a relationship with you. This breeds loyalty and allows the work or personal environment to be enjoyable. It is important to know that team leadership does not necessarily indicate multiple people. Team can mean two people. However, the emphasis is on interpersonal relationships with others. It is the phase of your self-awareness that allows you to reach out to others to develop friendships or working relationships.

Be aware that this rung on the ladder is not about how others are responding to you but it is about becoming aware of how you respond to others. In other words, it is about you choosing to invest in the lives of others. It is taking the time to get to know those around you on a personal level. We tend to use the excuse that in my work environment it is not "professional" to invest in others. Nothing could be further from the truth. If we are to successfully influence others through accountability then we must be accountable to invest in those around us. Choosing to learn about those we work and live with is essential if we are going to influence others.

Take a moment to think about someone with whom you have a professional or even personal relationship. Have you taken the time to invest in this person's life? Do you know about their family? How about a struggle they are currently facing? Have you taken the time to discover things that make this person unique? Obviously, your investment looks different from the perspective of a co-worker versus a personal friend. However the concept is essentially the same. Are you choosing to invest in those around you?

Many times we allow our fear to keep us from developing a relationship with those around us. Being self aware of our fear and reaching out to develop powerful relationships is the key to successfully influencing others. Keep in mind that simply choosing to become a team leader does not mean that everything will go smoothly. There will be those that reject you, there will be others that avoid you and there will be those who are simply rude and arrogant toward you. Once again, leading effectively is not contingent on how others respond to you; it is based on your self-awareness of choosing to invest in others.

Once you've made the conscious choice to invest in the lives of others and lead on the team leadership rung of the ladder, you will notice that your relationships are growing and becoming stronger. However staying on the team level of the leadership ladder will breed mediocrity with those around you. In other words, there is more to leading yourself well than simply developing relationships.

Task Leadership

The third rung on the leadership ladder is the Task leadership level. On this level you begin to hold yourself accountable for the task at hand. Your influence becomes results driven and others will follow you because of your ability to accomplish the task. The Task leadership level is not contingent upon IQ alone. It is the ability use EQ and IQ together in order to achieve the task at hand. When this occurs, momentum begins to build and tangible outcomes are experienced.

For years, the Task leadership level was the sole criteria for investments within corporate America. Someone was deemed a top performer solely based on his or her ability to accomplish the task. Subsequently, this person was placed in a leadership role based on their IQ alone. The result was the creation of a leadership or management team of highly intelligent people with very little ability to navigate a team or truly influence others. This philosophy works well if your product is the "only game in town" and you do not have to compete against others or build strategic relationships to ensure success. That certainly is not the case in today's global economy. Businesses and organizations that figured out the EQ secret first are those who rose to the top from the perspective of employee satisfaction and the financial profit and loss statement.

I work with an organization that is very task driven. They market their ability to "solve hard problems". The team is comprised of highly intelligent scientists, engineers, and technicians. However, they realize the importance of EQ and developed a culture that not only focuses on accomplishment of the task but also the development of their people. The leadership team is committed to being intentional about building a culture that is people centered, yet results driven. Their reputation is stellar and they are among the top in their industry in terms of work environment, employee satisfaction, and client satisfaction. Consequently, they have experienced a sustained trajectory of growth, and they are projected to continue that upward trend. Clearly their leaders have developed strategic relationships both internally and externally while continuing to focus on accomplishing the tasks that provide the revenue for a successful business venture.

At the Task level, you become self-aware of your position, choose to invest in those around you, while pursuing the tangible outcomes that are expected in any organization. However, be aware that staying on the Task level of the leadership ladder may cause us to lose sight of relationships. Remember short-term results are not the end goal. If we are going to sustain growth we must understand the next rung on the leadership ladder.

Teach Leadership

Climbing the leadership ladder is not for cowards. It is a difficult journey with constant struggles and failures along with successes along the way. The fourth rung on the ladder may be the most important level of all. This level includes investing in others from an educational standpoint as well as a personal standpoint. It is where mentoring, coaching, and teaching come into play. This is the level of long-term growth for not only yourself but for those that you are influencing. This is the differentiating factor for organizations that sustain long periods of growth and those that do not.

There has been much written about mentoring and coaching in recent days. This is a direct result of the awareness of EQ and the importance of passing along intangible bits of wisdom, experience and education to those around us. It is critical for any personal or professional relationship, that we are aware of our need to learn from others and that we recognize the importance of teaching others. This process can come through years of investment or in the spontaneity of a powerful moment.

Jim Collins, the author of *Good to Great* and other powerful leadership books, was asked about the importance of mentors in his life. He shares the following advice he got from others: "John Gardner (Secretary of Health, Education, and Welfare) told me. 'Don't try to be interesting - be interested.'" Another one came from a close friend. "There are 2 approaches to view life: either as a transaction or as a relationship. But only those who go at it as relationship can have a great life. Because life is about people and about relationship." The last one came from Peter Drucker. "Don't worry about trying to survive, don't worry about trying to be successful, focus on trying be useful."

The process of reaching the Teach leadership level of self-awareness begins with our acknowledgement that we still have much to learn about life. No matter what age we find ourselves, no matter what experience level we possess, choosing to be "interested" in developing ourselves on multiple levels is the key to being successful at the teach leadership level. This awareness allows us to authentically make ourselves available to teach others as we learn.

Organizations who choose to invest in developing leaders are those who enjoy a deep well of talent within their ranks. This can only occur when their employees choose to invest in each other. It must happen on every level through the organizational structure from the C suite to the entry-level team members. Everyone has something to contribute to the process of education. Because we all have a unique history, background and experience, we house valuable information and perspective for those with whom we live and work.

Choosing to invest in others by our knowledge and experience must come with an unconditional regard for others. In other words, we must realize that our teaching may fall on deaf ears, may be met with sarcasm or resentment, or may not be validated at all. That is not our responsibility and we must not become discouraged. Instead we must search for those who are willing to learn. Our responsibility is to offer mentorship, coaching and education to those who are willing to receive and apply our teaching.

Take a moment to ask yourself the hard question: Who am I teaching at this time in my life?

This person could be 88 or 8. They could work on the assembly line or in serve in C suite. They could be our neighbor or coworker. Using our knowledge or skill set to teach others is the highest level on the Leadership ladder that we can achieve independently. However, there is one more level on the Leadership ladder.

TOTAL LEADERSHIP

Total leadership is the highest rung on the leadership ladder. It is a role in which others place you, due to their respect and recognition of your ability to inspire and lead effectively. Those who have achieved the total leadership level are there because others have placed them there. In other words we reach the Total leadership level because of the investment we have made in Title level, Team level, Task level, and Teach level of influence in the lives of others. Only when we are self-aware of our responses on each of these levels can we hope to obtain the Total leadership level.

LEADERSHIP LADDER

Total leadership can take place on a macro or micro level. There are those in our society who have made significant contributions and have impacted the lives of thousands and thousands of people. When you think of total leaders on a global level you might think of persons such as Gandhi, Mother Teresa, Nelson Mandela, or Martin Luther King.

Likewise, we have Total leaders who have impacted our lives personally. Take a moment to think about individuals who are Total leaders in your life. Think about those who have played a role in leading you from a Title, Team, Task, and Teach perspective. These individuals have influenced you, led you, invested in you, taught you, and clearly influenced who you are today.

My personal goal is to lead with authenticity and vulnerability so that I might become a Total leader and ultimately make a difference in the lives of others.

One more word about the Leadership Ladder; the process is fluid. We are constantly going up and down the Leadership Ladder in our personal and professional relationships. Sometimes I operate out of the Title mentality and have to hold myself accountable to continue to progress up the leadership ladder to a different level. Other times I find myself making progress and moving up the ladder in order to lead others more effectively. The secret is to have the self-awareness to know where we are on the Leadership Ladder at any given time in our lives and in various circumstances.

Chapter Five
Self-Management

The second component that leads to understanding emotional intelligence is gaining the ability to manage oneself. We call this self-management. It is using the awareness of your emotions to stay flexible and direct your behavior positively. This means managing your emotional reactions to situations and people.

In order to successfully achieve self-management, we must be intentional, disciplined, and practice self-control. This can be incredibly difficult in both personal and professional relationships. Self-management takes adaptability and flexibility when controlling our behavior. This means we must take the initiative to make a conscientious effort to manage our verbal and nonverbal behavior toward others. It means knowing when to allow our emotions to provide a thoughtful response and knowing when to allow our emotions to drive a more intense response. This means at times we must be patient and at other times we must be urgent.

Mastering the self-management component of EQ takes practice, hard work, and commitment.

Understanding how our brain works might help us to gain the tools to master the self-management component of EQ. As I mentioned earlier, the Amygdala area of the brain is where our emotions are formed and expressed. The executive reasoning area can be found in the frontal cortex of the brain. These two areas are in constant battle with each other to provide perspective, reaction and interpretation of the events surrounding us.

For instance, if we see a child about to enter a busy intersection, our Amygdala sends us an urgent message to rush to rescue the child. While the executive reasoning portion of the brain may try to convince us of the danger we are putting ourselves in, it is most likely that the Amygdala will win this battle and thus we would rush to save the child even at the expense of our own life. Conversely, if we are considering a financial investment opportunity with risk involved, our Amygdala may push us to make a decision impulsively, while our executive reasoning would have us take the time necessary to research and thoroughly investigate such an investment risk. I would hope that our Executive Reasoning would win this battle and we would thus do our due diligence of research before jumping into the investment opportunity.

In order to help us to better understand these processes, consider the Wise Mind approach.

We will use the following diagram to illustrate this tool. The wise mind concept is about achieving balance between one's emotional thoughts and one's logical or executive reasoning thoughts. Psychology researcher, Marsha Linehan, Ph.D., at the

University of Washington, developed the wise mind concept. When we become out of balance in our thinking or behavior we lose the ability to self manage. This out of balance can look like being too logical or too emotional. Either extreme way of thinking causes division and can hinder communication. Yet, when there is a balance between these two ways of thinking, logic and emotion unite, and we have what is called a "wise mind" response.

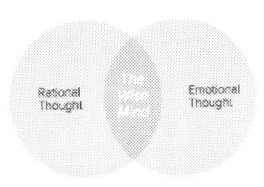

The person who allows his logical thought process or executive reasoning to rule might appear to lack "feelings" or appear to explain himself as if everything is a matter of common sense. He may appear to disconnect from people easily or not worry about problems others consider to be upsetting. This logical approach would likely be more obvious when dealing with problems. This logical approach can work well with problem solving—unless it is concerning relationship problems—then it can sound cold and uncaring to some.

The person who allows her emotional Amygdala side to rule might appear to be overly sensitive or emotional when confronted or held accountable. She might tend to respond impulsively to certain situations and could be seen as having a knee jerk reaction to the problem at hand. The emotional or Amygdala response is appropriate when dealing with compassion and concern for others. It can work well with problem solving when people are involved in the process. When it is out of balance it may place too much importance on the feelings of others.

Let's look at a personal scenario of Angela and Michael's relationship for example. They had been dating for about six months when Michael made a comment about feeling a little smothered by her at times, explaining that he had missed out on some activities with his friends because of all the time they were spending together. Angela was affectionate and a little clingy at times, but it was only because she loved to be with Michael and loved to talk with him. This translated into multiple calls to Michael each day and either her coming over to his apartment every evening or asking him to come to hers. In her mind, it was assumed all weekends would be spent together at this point in their relationship. Consequently, when Michael made the comment about feeling a little "smothered" by her, she felt he was rejecting her and was about to end the relationship. To make matters worse, this had happened to her in the past. Her response was to become emotionally upset and start crying as if he were ending the relationship.

Michael was confused by her response. It didn't seem logical. He did not want to break off their relationship; he just wanted more time for some activities with the guys. The problem was, he was irritated and was feeling the relationship was a little confining. Not being good with words, and having thought he had already clearly hinted that he wanted to do some things with his friends without her coming along, he blurted out, "You're smothering me!" To Michael, Angela's response was not logical or rational and he could not see the problem. Maybe he should not have yelled at her, but he was simply telling her the way he felt and what he wanted. It was simple. It was logical—at least to him. To Angela, his words were insensitive and rejecting. Michael was not a bad guy. He really liked Angela and did not want to end the relationship. It was just that his logical mind, or rational thought process, caused him to speak without considering how she might possibly feel about his words.

Let's consider a professional example of two people at odds with one another at work. These two people are involved in an argument over how to proceed on a project and neither is willing to give an inch. In fact, it seems they are unable to resolve their differences no matter how long they argue. In this scenario the problem is that Bryan, an engineer, is arguing his point with Carmen, a business major. Bryan is a good employee and has accomplished many difficult tasks at the company. He generally operates solely from the executive reasoning or logical mind. Carmen feels like he ignores her input and has a pattern of not listening to what she has to say. She believes that he just wants to "solve the problem" with no concern for how it may affect other areas of the organization. Bryan does not understand why some people (especially Carmen) get so emotional about things that he sees as illogical. Situations, ideas and actions are either right or they are wrong. The problem is black and white and he cannot understand why Carmen is so concerned about how projects affect others in a negative way. After all, that is not his issue; he is there to solve problems. The fallout from his work is not his concern.

Carmen wants Bryan to understand that he needs to consider the feelings and circumstances of others. She is passionate about her feelings on the subject and accuses him of sounding and responding like a robot. The more emotional she becomes the more logical he becomes, pushing them farther and farther apart.

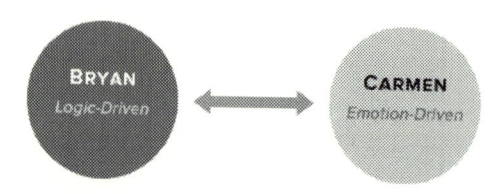

BRYAN *Logic-Driven* ⟷ **CARMEN** *Emotion-Driven*

The only way to find a balanced perspective is for Bryan to cease to hold on to a purely logic-driven perspective and to be open to hearing what Carmen has to say as well as to take the time to consider her perspective. This simple act will help prevent them from moving farther apart. This does not mean he will have to accept something that is illogical or that doesn't make sense, but it does mean he will have to be willing to see the value of her perspective and why it is important for the overall good of the company.

Likewise, Carmen will need to stop moving away from Bryan by holding on to an emotionally driven perspective and consider the logic Bryan brings to the discussion. Just by seriously considering his perspective, she begins to move toward him. As both continue to work to see the other's perspective, neither has to give up his or her perspective. Just the same, a natural overlapping of perspectives or "minds" will occur, producing what is called the "wise mind." This is where the balance takes place. Ideas become reasonable and people become agreeable. Ideally, the need for control or to have one's way or to "win the argument" is done away with as each person respects the other's perspective.

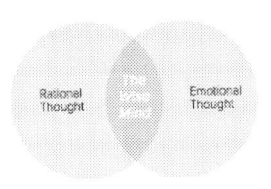

The discipline of using the wise-mind process begins with becoming self aware of how we are addressing a situation or circumstance. Once we define if we are operating out of the Amygdala or the Executive Reasoning area of the brain we can then make a conscious choice of responding in the appropriate manner.

If self-management sounds like a lot of work, that's because it does take a lot of work to successfully manage our behavior. However, the reward of learning to manage our emotions and behavior is well worth the effort. Those who make a practice of executing self-management principles find that their relationships are more successful. This includes leading a team, engaging with a coworker, or developing a long-lasting relationship with those we love.

Chapter Six
Social Awareness

Once we have gained the ability to become self-aware and begun the process of managing our own emotions and behavior we are ready to turn our attention toward social awareness. Social awareness is the ability to accurately pick up on other people's emotions and understand what is really going on with them. A majority of miscommunication occurs because a person inaccurately reads the emotional intent of someone else. That is why the number one issue in team development is communication. In our personal lives and in our professional lives we all struggle to communicate effectively.

In the context of communicating with others, creating clarity is largely our responsibility. However, being understood does not necessarily take place because one speaks clearly or gives clear instructions. There is much more to communicating than this. Think about communicating one piece of information to a coworker. The following questions must be interpreted correctly for the communication to be a success:

- What did I say?
- Did I say what I meant to say?

- Did he hear what I said?
- Did he hear what I meant to say?
- Did my nonverbal signs support my verbal communication?
- Did he understand my intent?
- Did he understand my content?

Hence the questions could go on and on.

Effective communication begins with working to prevent misunderstandings. A good place to begin is by clarifying the message we are communicating and the message being communicated to us. Here are three steps for clarifying communication:

Step 1: Clarify your message by speaking the unspoken thought or assumed intent. In other words, don't assume the person with whom you are communicating fully understands what you are trying to say. This is especially true when we are speaking with people with whom we are familiar or have a great deal of interaction. We may assume they know what we mean when, in fact, they do not. Say all you mean as if the person is not familiar with your likes and dislikes or preferred method. Also, you might want to let them know what you're hoping to accomplish or the reason you are telling them something. It does not have to be a long conversation; just include all the information needed when making your request, comment, or point.

Step 2: Clarify your message by asking the other person if your comment or directions were understood. The fact is we do not always communicate as effectively as we think. Just as with the previous step, we are looking for missing information or vague perception. Therefore, it is often a good idea to ask the person, in a way that doesn't sound arrogant, if he or she understands the point you were trying to make or your intent. Most won't ask many follow-up questions, so take the responsibility to clarify your message with the other person.

Step 3: When you have a plan, work to make sure everyone is on board by clarifying everyone's intent. Great plans often go wrong because everyone was not on board. To make matters worse, people are often passive-aggressive, meaning they will act and say one thing but feel and do something else. Because of this, one should not assume everyone is going to be on board with your plan just because no one complained about it.

Communicating effectively is something that takes constant attention and work. Learning to become socially aware will help us in our endeavor to communicate to those around us. In order for us to become socially aware, we must be intuitive of how other people are reacting and responding to the conversation, circumstances, or environment. This means we must develop empathy toward others. Social awareness begins with an authentic concern for those around us. Listening is a key component of developing strong social awareness. Developing an understanding of opposing views is a critical piece to solving the social awareness puzzle. Keep in mind that understanding someone's view is not the same as agreeing with someone's view. Stephen Covey, a renowned author and leadership guru said that we must "seek first to understand". This is a wonderful example of growing our EQ by increasing our social awareness.

Many times we find ourselves having a unilateral approach when it comes to the environment around us. In other words we develop in our mind what we think the answer should be and begin to make assumptions around the answer before taking the time to truly become aware of the truth. This approach causes division and polarization within relationships, businesses, and culture. Choosing to develop an empathetic mindset is a defining characteristic in powerful and effective leaders. It is easy to think of accountability as a one-way street. That, however, is not accountability but rather dictatorship.

Accountability begins with connection. It is vital to connect with the person or persons with whom you wish to influence. In his book, *Everyone Communicates, Few Connect,* John Maxwell says, "Connecting is the ability to identify with people and relate to them in a way that increases your influence with them."

Connecting to influence is the essence of REAL accountability. We are most influenced by people with whom we have a connection. We care about what they think or say because we have a relationship with them. This is why the opinion of a total stranger means very little, but the opinion of a parent, close friend or mentor means a great deal. Just as we have people in our life who influence us, we have the same opportunity to influence others.

Let's look at what it will take for others to be willing to open themselves up to our influence in their lives. John Maxwell tells us more about connecting with others when he observes that there are, "Three questions people are asking about you":

1. "Do you care for me?"
2. "Can you help me?"
3. "Can I trust you?"

If we can adequately answer these three questions in regards to those with whom we are looking to connect and communicate, we will likely have the opportunity to influence them in the future.

Be aware that the scope of these questions is not limited to leading and influencing coworkers and friends. People in every area of your life will ask these questions of you. Anyone in your sphere of influence, can and will ask these questions in a hundred different ways. Take a look at the meaning behind these critical questions:

- *"Do you care for me?"* : In other words, "Do you think of me? Are you concerned about me? Will you take time for me? Am I important to you?"
- *"Can you help me?"*: "Will you take the time to lift me up? Are you interested in seeing me succeed? Do you have something to offer me?"
- *"Can I trust you?"*: Asked another way, "Will you hurt me? Will you disappoint me? Can I depend on you to be there for me when I need you?

Answering these powerful questions for those around us will allow for connection on a level that leads to influencing through accountability.

Likewise, sharpening our listening skills, using self-awareness and self-management to discover opposing views and bring balance to a diverse opinion group, will lead to strong social awareness. Choosing to influence by connecting with others will ultimately lead to raising our EQ.

In an effort to provide a way to practically apply the EQ discipline, allow me to introduce a tool that we call Triple A. It is designed to serve as an easy to use model for increasing our social awareness.

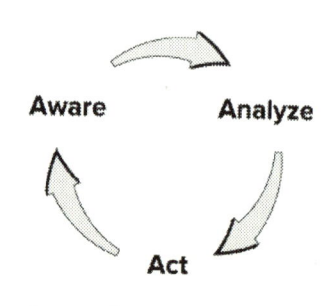

Aware   Analyze

Act

AWARE - ANALYZE - ACT MODEL

In this model, the key feature is seeing there is a process that can lead us to becoming more aware of others and ourselves. Allow me to explain the three steps to this process.

1. When faced with a decision or difficult circumstance, slow down and take a moment to become **aware** of what is happening and what is at stake. Consider yourself, but also consider others, and what is going on around you or what is at stake.
2. Next, **analyze** your thoughts about what you are considering to do in response to the situation. Ask

yourself, "Is this the best thing for me to do or say? What is the best response? Could I handle this differently?" In short, question yourself. Think it through. Do not just react.
3. Finally, when you **act**, make sure what you have chosen to do will lead to the greatest good. Some situations cannot be handled in a way that everyone is happy or in a way that everything ends up being perfect. Go for the greater good—the right thing—the best choice.

It is interesting to note that the AAA model can be accessed from anywhere with in the AAA cycle. For instance, if you find yourself impulsively acting, you can begin the process by taking a step back, becoming aware and then analyzing your current behavior. If you find yourself over analyzing a situation you can use the model to stimulate action. If you're simply assessing a relationship or situation you can start with the aware phase and work your way around the cycle to action.

Triple A can be used in an effective way to increase your social awareness. This simple tool can be quickly memorized and practically applied in a variety of settings and circumstances. It helps you to quickly navigate to the wise mind area with in your decision-making process.

The final component of the EQ equation is relationship management. Let's take a look at how we can begin to effectively navigate our important relationships.

Chapter Seven
Relationship Management

Relationship management is using the awareness of your emotions and those of others to manage interactions successfully. True influence occurs with the ability to successfully manage our relationships through difficult times. Relationship management does not occur quickly and takes commitment to invest in the lives of others.

Becoming socially aware and listening to the needs of others simply isn't enough. Navigating strategic relationships both externally and internally in an organization is critical to the lifecycle of that entity. Relationship management may take the form of employee development, teambuilding exercises, or learning about conflict resolution. It includes giving and receiving constructive feedback and giving others the opportunity to influence you. Relationship management is not a one-way street. It is the giving and receiving that occurs within any healthy relationship.

A person who is skilled in relationship management is knowledgeable in people interactions. Consequently, he has gained the tools to use his skill effectively. Some might believe that when it comes to building relationships, either someone has that skill, or they don't, and there's not much that can change it. That simply is not true. We have found that successfully interacting with people and building relationships is a skill much like anything else. Some have a natural tendency to excel relationally, due to life experiences or personality, but all can learn the skill of building and managing relationships that will last and be fulfilling. The question is, are we willing to invest the time and discipline to master this skill?

Those who are mastering the relationship management skill are those who are operating in the Teach level of the Leadership ladder and even the Total leadership Ladder level. This is where true inspiration occurs.

It is true however that there are different levels of relationship management. Understanding the different levels of relationship is important to managing and interacting with others.

Accountability serves to build trust and stability in business and personal relationships. When we are accountable to others, and they to us, we learn whom we can trust and how to build trust. For example, if I know I can depend on you or you know you can depend on me because of our past experience with one another, we have a mutual trust. Conversely, when someone demonstrates by their past experiences, that they are not trust worthy, the relationship will be damaged.

This trust and stability is equally important in the business arena. Accountability among coworkers will strengthen the morale of the group and make each a stronger team player. To put it plainly, others knowing "you have their back" or that you will stand with them and struggle toward success with them is what I mean when I encourage you to be accountable to those with whom you work. In this kind of atmosphere, no one is seeking his own good above that of another.

The following illustration represents the different levels of relationships existing between others and us. This is relevant in our personal and business relationships. However, for our purposes we will focus on the business relationship model.

LEVELS OF RELATIONAL SHARING

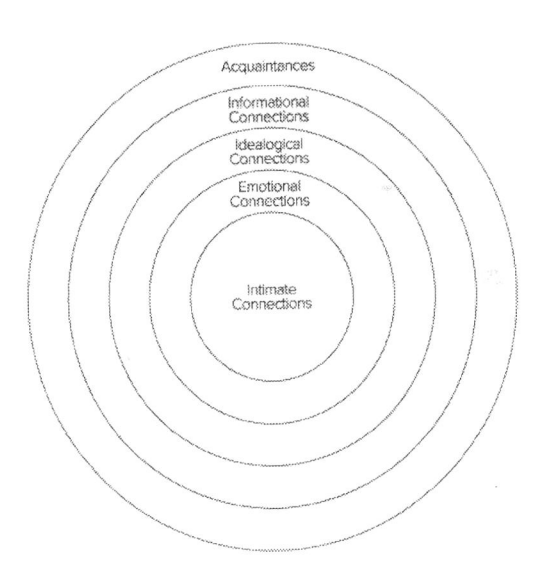

- Acquaintances
- Informational Connections
- Ideaological Connections
- Emotional Connections
- Intimate Connections

The first level, represented by the outer ring, represents those people who are only business acquaintances. These are people we come in contact with, and know only from a distance.

59

The second level, represented by the next ring, we have those people who are our business associates. These are the people with whom we collaborate and solve problems.

The third level, we begin to develop a sense of trust in our business relationships. There is a sense of confidentiality and a common desire to accomplish goals.

The fourth level, we develop a stronger trust and awareness that we can generally depend on these people

Finally, **the fifth level** (center circle), are those very few people that we have developed a past experience of deep trust. This level is developed through time and experiencing struggles together.

Social-awareness occurs when we realize the level of each of our relationships. Think of relationship management as an emotional swinging gate. On levels one and two the gate is only open a slight amount. We are polite yet protected. We realize that we must remain closed to deep emotional connections or feelings. As the relationship develops and the levels increase to three, four and five, the gate opens wider. Consequently, the relationship deepens and we become more vulnerable. This means that as trust increases, we gain the ability to share authentic, honest thoughts and feelings as well as the ability to offer sincere feedback to each other.

While I have referred to a personal relationship, professional relationships track the same process. The business relationships that are centered on mutual trust and admiration are those that are the most successful. It is critical for any professional to understand the relationship level for each strategic partner in which they engage business practices. Likewise it is important internally for organizations to understand the level on which each of their team members operate. The most effective leadership teams are those who have walked through struggles together and have developed a level four or five relationship.

Influencing others through accountability means that as business professionals, we must conduct ourselves in such a way as to empower those around us. Instead of seeking to outshine our co-workers, we should look for a way to help them shine. It is our responsibility to influence by serving. When we commit to manage our relationships with integrity we will see incredible changes occur on our professional teams and in our personal lives. Remember that relationship management is a two way street. While others may depend on us to do our best, we must also trust them to do their best.

In order for effective relationship management to take place we must understand the continuum of aggressive, assertive, and passive interactions.

Not everyone finds it easy to be assertive in relationships. At times this may take the form of someone's being unable to stand up for her rights and at other times, the same person may explode in anger, becoming overly aggressive. Neither of these actions or reactions is a healthy response. Being assertive is essentially standing up for your rights without violating someone else's rights. The question, however, is how does one do that when she has no experience with being assertive?

Allow me to explain the basics of being assertive in one's communication and behavior in a healthy way. Consider the diagram below, which represents a continuum or range of communication styles and behaviors, from the extremes of passive behavior to that of aggressive behavior. We have placed assertive communication and behavior in the middle of our continuum to represent healthy or productive behavior.

PASSIVE - ASSERTIVE - AGGRESSIVE CONTINUUM

Passive
(Lose/Win)

Assertive
(Win/Win)

Aggressive
(Win/Lose)

Let's develop a clear understanding of what we mean by each of these terms and how someone can navigate the span of human reactions that we have often encountered in our interaction with others. Our goal is to avoid ending up in either of the extreme areas mentioned.

- The **passive** individual is usually not the best communicator of her feelings. In fact, she may say she feels one way, but act as if she feels another. We call that being passive-aggressive. She is nice, but at the same time she appears hostile. It's like she is holding in her feelings. Sometimes the passive individual may come across as too nice or too accommodating. She may allow people to take advantage of her "good nature." Often, part of the problem is that she feels guilty saying no to others' requests.

- On the other end of the continuum is the **aggressive** individual. The aggressive person is easy to spot. She is the one nobody wants to cross or make angry. She already appears to be angry or a little ticked off most of the time. If she has to, she will threaten, manipulate, use guilt, or explode in order to get her way. There is no doubt she is in control and everyone plays by her rules. In short, she's mean!
- Now that we have been to each extreme, let's gets some balance and go to the middle of the continuum to the **assertive** individual. Either of the previously mentioned individuals would conduct themselves completely different if they were simply being assertive. As an assertive person, this lady would be firm in her response. Her yes would mean yes, and her no would mean no. Likewise she would say what she meant when asked and you would not wonder if she was expressing her true feelings or just trying to please you. She would allow you to disagree with her without having an emotional "meltdown" because you disagreed. If someone tried to push their opinion or wants on her, she could stand her ground and hold on to her boundaries without feeling the need to clash with the other person.

In reality, most people will find themselves at different places on the continuum from time to time. I have not met the person who can live perfectly in the middle of the continuum at all times. We all know someone living at either end of the continuum in the area of extreme behavior.

Consider the following practical suggestions for being assertive in your conversations and behavior:

1. **Use "I" statements.** Beginning your conversation by pointing out what you feel is much safer and more productive than beginning with an accusation, such as, "I don't know what YOUR problem is, but..." Or "YOU need to sit down and listen! I am angry about what YOU have done." This is aggressive. The conversation starts off much better when we calmly start with a comment such as the following: "Do you remember what happened yesterday when I got upset? Well, I was feeling like..." Followed by: "I need you to help me in the future by remembering..."
2. **Focus on behaviors.** We may feel like we can read minds or that we know someone so well we know what he or she is thinking at times, but this is almost always a mistake when having those tough conversations. Instead of making statements about another's motives, feelings, attitude, or thought processes, stick to what you know for sure—what they did. If your issue is with someone's actions or behavior, speak directly to it. Motives, feelings, attitude, or thought processes can always be disputed, but actions are more concrete.

For example, let's say you have a coworker who likes to hang out in your office. You like him and he could be considered a friend. The problem is that he doesn't seem to understand good boundaries and is prone to intruding into your space or conversations with others. For some time now you have allowed, or tolerated, him dropping in for visits that seem to last for an hour or more. Your subtle hints don't work. Your non-verbal gestures don't work. If you choose to allow this to continue you can see yourself beginning to dislike this fellow and it becoming difficult to work with him. So, how do you assert yourself and prevent him from taking advantage of your good nature?

To begin with, don't get caught up in a conversation that sounds something like this: "Jay! What's your problem? Why are you bothering me? Don't you have work to do?" All Jay will hear is your calling him lazy and that you don't like him. The conversation will go downhill fast from here.

Instead, focus on the behavior that is the problem by responding to his entrance into your office and saying something like this: "Hey, Jay! Can you give me a few minutes? I would really like to talk but I am swamped with work. How about we get lunch and catch up?" Alternatively, perhaps you could reverse the setting by saying, "Hey Jay, let me finish this and I will swing by your office in a little while." It will be easier for you to control the time you spend with Jay if you become the visitor to his office and he will still feel important to you.

3. **Keep your responses brief.** No need to address everything someone says in his response to your comments or requests. For example, he may respond angrily to you standing your ground by accusing you and responding, "That's not fair!" At this point he could

take the conversation off course if you follow his logic. Stick to the point. The point is, you told him not to do something and he did it. He violated your trust and did not respect your request. Nothing else should be brought into this conversation.

4. **Watch your tone of voice and non-verbal messages.** It's a proven truth that if you start a conversation calmly, it is very likely you will end the conversation calmly. Of course, speaking calmly while gritting your teeth and firing death rays from your eyes is not the same. Your facial expressions and body language need to match your calm voice. Without talking down to the person or sounding like a parent scolding a child, just say what you have to say in a normal tone of voice.

5. **Listen to what others are saying.** Once you have made your point, stop and listen to what the other person has to say. Listening is a great way of learning about others' point of view. If the person makes a point worth considering—consider it. If not, just listen. You do not have to change your mind or agree—just listen. Once the person has finished speaking, acknowledge what he said and, if not swayed, take him back to the issue at hand.

6. **Maintain appropriate eye contact.** Appropriate eye contact will depend on the person. People from certain cultures or backgrounds may view constant, direct eye contact as aggressive or as an attempt to intimidate. However, as a rule it is best to look at someone when he is talking to you or you to him. Looking away, or down, while talking to someone is often considered rude or can be interpreted as having something to hide.

As you practice these techniques you will begin to find it easier and easier to be assertive. It will become more comfortable and you will see that you do not need to give in to please others or stand your ground like it's a battle for life or death. Instead, as you practice these techniques, you will find it possible to agree to disagree in an agreeable fashion.

There are times when relationship management equals having difficult conversations. Conflict is inevitable and resolving it requires ongoing work if it is to be resolved for the good of all involved. As mentioned in *Make A Difference*, the first volume of this series, "One of the key ingredients to successfully navigating relationships is the ability to deal with conflict in a healthy manner. Generally, when we think of conflict, it brings a negative connotation to our mind. That is, we have negative mental pictures associated with the word conflict. However, all healthy teams and all healthy relationships must have conflict. Believe it or not, conflict is a good thing as long as it is navigated effectively. It gives us the ability to authentically share our feelings, provide input from different perspectives, and create ownership and accountability."

In light of this, those who lead and influence others must realize conflict is, to some degree, essential and therefore we must develop our ability and skills in the area of conflict resolution. In fact, successfully navigating conflict is one of the more effective ways we influence others. Now that we have a good understanding of how to assert ourselves in a positive manner, let's consider various conversations most will encounter from time to time and how we can navigate them in the best possible way.

Is there anything that sends a feeling of dread through our being like someone calmly pulling us aside and saying, "We need to talk."? Impending doom just seems to hover above us! Chances are, what follows is not going to make us happy. We can sense the disappointment coming our way. We draw back, assuming we have done something wrong and we are about to be corrected or chastised. Unfortunately, those difficult conversations are a reality of life and at some point everyone will either be called aside or call someone else aside to have that talk. However, having those difficult conversations doesn't have to cause us a sense of dread. Difficult conversations can have a positive outcome. Whether we are initiating the talk or we are the focus of the talk, we can learn to have that conversation in the best possible way.

The essential conversation is that conversation that has to take place for the good of the relationship. It is the one we often put off until later. It's the conversation with no easy solutions and no way to say what's needed without the other person's becoming unhappy. It's the one we dread—the one we feel uncomfortable having to have with someone. It is the conversation that must take place.

Crucial Conversations: Tools for talking when stakes are high is a book that offers a great deal of help in this area. While it is impossible to briefly summarize all the valuable knowledge the authors offer, allow me to highlight some basics from the book that are central to our discussion. Let's begin by defining what is meant by a "crucial conversation." A crucial conversation is a discussion between two or more people where "stakes are high, opinions vary, and emotions run strong." These conversations may take various forms, such as:

- addressing someone's rude or offensive behavior
- assessing a coworker's performance
- talking to an uncommitted team member
- disagreeing with a friend over something that is upsetting to him/her
- breaking up with someone you've been dating

In order to have these essential conversations in the best possible way, let's turn our attention to three straightforward steps the authors give us that we can take in having our conversation. Allow me to summarize:

1. **Start with safety.** Eliminate the unknown. Clearly explain the issue. Get to the point, but do it in a way the other person does not feel threatened or attacked. This is done by showing respect for the other person in words, actions, and even facial expressions. Respect is the key component. If a person feels threatened or demeaned he will not feel it is safe to communicate and will likely respond defensively by shutting down or attacking.

2. **Share your path.** Start with the facts and stay with the facts. Don't fall into the trap of assigning meaning to another's actions or stating you know what the other person meant or was thinking. This will help to keep emotion out of the conversation or at a minimum and prevent the person from feeling attacked. State what you saw or what you heard and be open to the possibility you may have misunderstood. If the person

still appears defensive, pause and help her to feel safe in communicating with you.
3. **End with a question.** A good question at this point will help you come to an understanding. A question such as, "What's your problem?" would only cause the person to become defensive or verbally retaliate. By asking something like, "What happened?" or "Can you tell me what's going on?" you make it safe for the other person to present her perspective. Hearing and understanding the other person's point of view is essential—even if you disagree with her. Allow the other person to ask questions and share her opinion or thoughts. By maintaining an open mind and a problem-solving approach you can navigate confrontation without it causing a relationship to be destroyed.

There are times when managing a relationship means dealing with someone who is reacting from emotional or irrational state of mind.

Imagine you are sitting in your office quietly working and your manager comes into your office. He is trying to control his voice and feelings, but he's obviously angry and apparently blaming you for the project not being finished—although you were held up by him dragging his feet on making a crucial decision pertaining to the project. Your first reaction might well be to give him a piece of your mind. After all, you alone are not responsible for the project being completed. It is supposed to be a team effort with him leading the team. The problem, however, is that your manager is already on the verge of freaking out and obviously angrier than a person should be about a project not being finished. If you respond by shouting back and accusing him of running you behind by his lack of action, things will only get worse. You know, because this is not the first time this has happened. The last time you reacted with an angry response, things got out of hand quickly. So, what do you do? You seek to diffuse the situation rather than attack or set him straight. To do this, consider the "Mr. Cola" method.

The "Mr. Cola" method for diffusing conflict is an object lesson, which can be used as a visual tool to help people understand how to navigate conflict when dealing with an irate person, and by irate, we mean very angry or enraged. It goes something like this. Imagine you have a bottle of cola in your hand and it represents a person who is prone to be explosive in nature. Now, shake the bottle of cola for a few seconds.

Now that you have shaken the bottle of cola you know the pressure has built up. It's ready to blow if you remove the top. This is why we chose the bottle of cola to represent that person with the explosive nature. He is reactive when he is upset. It might be something someone says or something someone does, that he does not like that upsets him. However, the pressure builds and builds. All you know is that when he is ready to blow, everyone wants to get away.

The question becomes, is this a person you want to confront when he is angry? Is he someone who will listen to your point of view? At that point, can you reason with him? The answer is no to all of the previous questions. He is like the bottle of cola. The best thing you can do with the bottle is to set it down and leave it alone for a while. Then, you can gently and slowly begin to ease the top off. With the bottle of cola, you will hear the pressurized air begin to escape. The bottle is decompressing. Allowed to decompress slowly, the pressure will be released completely and the top can be removed without consequence.

With the volatile person we must take a similar approach. After giving him time to calm down a bit, we can ease into a conversation with him in which he can express himself. He still may seem on the verge of exploding, but by maintaining a calm voice and demeanor we can guide him in decompressing. The purpose is not to let him rant until he runs out of steam, but to help him express himself in a productive manner. Drawing from various voices of experience I have complied several ways in which this can be done:

1. Be direct and specific with your concerns and expectations about his behavior.
2. Do not allow the conversation to escalate.
3. Don't blame, accuse, belittle, or lecture him.
4. It is okay for you to be angry about his behavior, but only if you remain composed.
5. Take a solution-oriented approach.
6. If you cannot be firm with him, you may become a victim of his anger.
7. Listen and ask questions about what he is saying.
8. Ask him to sit down and talk with you. You want him to feel you are genuinely listening so he does not feel the need to make you listen.
9. Once you have done this you can move to the problem-solving stage in which productive steps can be taken to solve any problems.

The important part of managing this situation is that you demonstrated a high level of EQ. You were self aware of how you were influencing the irate person and practiced self-management by staying in the wise mind. Then you were socially aware and used the Triple A cycle to develop and execute relationship management by operating in the assertive area of the emotional continuum. You listened with empathy and asked questions centered on problem solving and not personal attack.

The result may be that you agree to disagree, but by using EQ you set the stage for effectively coming to a positive resolution. Likewise you demonstrated an authentic respect for the individual. Relationship management begins and ends with being accountable to one another.

Developing respect and trust can be demonstrated by allowing others to surround you who have strengths in areas that you are weak. Likewise you demonstrate a willingness to use your strengths to compensate for others weaknesses. This give and take is the secret ingredient to relationship management. When we walk with one another in difficult times, we earn the right to influence. When we authentically celebrate the success of others we earn the right to hold them accountable.

In order to manage our significant relationships on a professional or personal level, we must start taking steps toward a more balanced way of thinking, communicating, and behaving. In other words, we must understand and execute the principle of leading with EQ as well as IQ.

Chapter Eight
Influence Through Validation and Affirmation

Accountability must be interfaced with validation and affirmation if we are to effectively influence others. Many times we confuse validation with manipulation.

The words we speak to those we seek to influence are important. No one can truly motivate another through manipulative comments. Remember, words that motivate are those that are aimed at sincerely investing in the other person. Manipulative words are self-serving, and are generally detected quickly by others. Manipulation can come in the form of an off-handed comment or a "back-handed" compliment. The comment usually sounds sarcastic or as if one is uninterested in other's accomplishments. The truth is, if we lack sincerity in our words they will be worthless to others. Furthermore, our words can sound meaningless if we fail to communicate in a way that person receives messages. In other words, certain words of praise and affirmation will mean little to someone if we are not speaking his or her language.

Using the REAL Accountability process, let's take a look at how each accountability style receives validation. Note that the accountability styles in this book correlate with the personality styles in the first book in this series, *Make A Difference*.

Relaters (extroverted, people-driven individuals) are validated, encouraged, and motivated by the approval and affirmation of others. They respond to kindness, warm thoughts, and genuine interest in them as a person. Words build them up or tear them down, so choose your words wisely. *Make A Difference* correlation – Monkey.

Executers (extroverted, task-driven individuals) are validated, encouraged, and motivated by respect, empowerment, and the accomplishment of the task. Executers will care more about whether or not you are impressed by their accomplishments than whether or not you are personally interested in them. *Make A Difference* correlation – Lion.

Analyzers (introverted, task-driven individuals) are validated, encouraged, and motivated through organized, detailed processes with an emphasis on the quality of the task. These people like to know you appreciate the effort they put into getting it right. Acknowledge their competence and you will affirm them. *Make A Difference* correlation – Camel.

Listeners (introverted, person-driven individuals) are validated, encouraged, and motivated when you focus on what is truly important – the significant relationships that they have established with those they love or with whom they are loyal. In other words, they value one-on-one interpersonal relationships. Take time with them and value their friendship and you will affirm them every time. *Make A Difference* correlation – Turtle.

Taking the time to validate others in this manner may seem to some as almost manipulating others with our words. Some would ask, "Why do I need to talk to people this way? Why can't I just say it like it is and let them deal with it?" The answer is simple: It's not all about you. Consequently, you will need to adjust your accountability approach to influence each individual's unique style. This is one of the reasons why understanding REAL Accountability is so important – it helps you to adjust your approach based on an actual understanding of that person and the way he or she hears and processes information.

For some, the idea of "affirming" others is outside of our comfort zone. Maybe we associate affirmation with manipulation. It is important to understand the difference. Manipulation has a self-gratifying agenda. Affirmation or validation has no agenda other than what is in the other person's or the organization's best interest. One's perspective and purpose is what defines the difference between manipulation and affirmation.

You may wonder how offering affirmation can positively influence others or if that is really even necessary for a good leader. We have heard it said that, if one is a good leader, people just follow that person naturally. That may be true. Some people may be "natural leaders". This could mean that they have a strong personality, a high competency in the area in which they are working, or a naturally high EQ. Regardless, they are still accountable for how they navigate and influence others.

Influencing others is about connecting. If you and I are going to be successful in our interactions with others, we must possess the skill to develop a positive interaction. Thus, learning to connect with others is essential and affirming them is one of the best methods for connecting. If we are supportive and dedicated to the good of others and their success, in most all cases we will find they will mirror our attitude and they will become supportive and loyal to us.

The bottom line is that no matter how we develop our leadership ability, choosing to connect and give accountability with validation and affirmation is a powerful way to influence others.

Chapter Nine
REAL Boundaries and Loyalty

In order to sustain accountability, we must understand and develop effective boundaries. This is true for our personal and professional lives. Regardless of our accountability style, each of us has a need for healthy boundaries in our lives.

Everyone has his or her personal limits and limitations. This is why boundaries are so important. Boundaries are those personal limits that define who we are and what we expect from others and ourselves. A boundary is about our right to say "yes" or "no" in a thousand different situations or to any number of questions. Healthy boundaries are essential to one's well being. Without our choosing to respect others' boundaries and they ours, we are destined to experience a violation of boundaries related to someone going too far in his actions or words.

Of course, boundaries are not primarily protective in nature. Boundaries instruct and guide in personal interaction, often facilitating positive experiences and progress toward goals. Likewise, boundaries set guidelines for a person's conduct, ethics, and other principles that guide one's life. Boundaries prevent hurt feelings and promote positive feelings. Usually, everyone involved feels better when personal boundaries are clear and respected.

Setting appropriate boundaries is vital in our personal lives as well as in our professional lives. Our personal boundaries allow us to grow and develop as adults. Ideally, learning to set healthy boundaries is part of the parenting process. Realistically, many homes do not practice or teach the skill of setting boundaries. The good news is that you can choose to begin the process of setting good boundaries regardless of where you are on your personal or professional journey. The result will yield more effective and meaningful personal relationships and we will experience much more success in our professional relationships.

The reality of boundaries is that they are much more about freedom and not just about limitations. Authors of several best selling books on relationships, Dr. Henry Cloud and Dr. John Townsend have this to say about the importance of boundaries: "Boundaries define us. They define what is me and what is not me. A boundary shows me where I end and someone else begins, leading me to a sense of ownership... Knowing what I am to own and take responsibility for gives me freedom." These are the principles that guide us in building and maintaining healthy relationships.

Influencing through REAL accountability is most effective when anchored in the foundation of strong personal and professional boundaries.

Make a Difference: Influence Through Accountability

Below is a simple tool that will help us to **"think"** as we set appropriate boundaries in our lives.

> **T** – Is it true? If one does not know a person's reported statement is accurate or a story told to them is true, it should not be repeated. It's as simple as that. Instead, the person who hears something about a friend, coworker, or acquaintance that is damaging to that person's reputation, should talk to the person in question and find out the truth instead of simply repeating it as if it were true.

> **H** – Is it helpful? This follows the previous guideline. When you are aware of something about someone else—even if it is true and even if it's not necessarily something bad—would sharing it be helpful? The question becomes not is it true? Rather how does it help that person? If we are accountable to others, we are concerned about their personal and professional welfare.

> **I** – Is it inspiring? Before speaking or making comments to others, we ask our self if what we are about to say is affirming or validating. Will our comments be something to help or motivate? Will our words make the other person better or worse? It's amazing how one can draw people to themselves by always pointing out something good about another person or something good about what he or she has done.

> **N** – Is it necessary? Do we really need to speak? Sometimes being quiet and listening provides a

powerful connection. Those who talk incessantly are generally those who are not respected or followed. In other words, "be slow to speak and quick to listen".

K – Is it kind? A simple reminder of how we truly influence others. Through genuine kindness we impact the lives of others. Consequently, a kind person will be a person who can influence and lead others.

Setting effective boundaries allows us to connect and influence. This sets the stage for a critical cornerstone of influencing through REAL accountability. If we are going to successfully experience the giving and receiving of accountability we must have a firm understanding of how to create loyalty.

People tend to find it easy to be loyal to others who have proven themselves to be honest, trustworthy, reliable, dependable, and committed. These qualities are gained through time and experience. The bottom line is that people are loyal to those they can trust. People will follow those they trust. Consequently, it is useless to attempt to lead or influence others if you cannot be trusted. People will never be loyal to a person who is inconsistent in his or her words and behavior. While they may like or even love that person, their ability to trust him simply will not be there.

If we desire to lead and influence others in a personal or professional environment, we have a responsibility to create loyalty. It will not just happen and cannot be passed down from another. It is not given through assuming or receiving a particular position. We must build it, generate it, produce it—through the way we live our lives.

REAL Accountability styles will each have a different perspective on how to execute appropriate boundaries. Likewise, each style will experience different struggles in accomplishing this goal. Here are some areas in which individual REAL Accountability styles may struggle:

Relaters may have a tendency to over-disclose. His boundaries may be too loose and open ended. This may look like giving personal information too quickly in a relationship. It may look like talking too much in a business meeting. The Relater will desire to connect quickly to others thus at times overreaching in the relationship. He needs to be aware of the possibility of over connecting and therefore, invalidating his credibility. His inclusive nature may cause him to over collaborate and lose the ability to influence through accountability.

Executers May have a tendency to not respect others' boundaries. She may be overly driven toward accomplishing the task and therefore overstep her bounds within her personal and professional relationships. The Executor will desire to move quickly and decisively causing others to feel left out and overlooked. She may speak with firm direct language and tone that could be interpreted as rude to others. She needs to be aware of her independent nature and slow down to include others in the process. Her lack of respect for another's boundary may cause her to lose the ability to influence through accountability.

Analyzers may have the tendency to set boundaries that are rigid and impenetrable. He lives in a black and white world; therefore there is no room for a pliable or flexible boundary. His need for hyper detailed data could damage relationships. The Analyzer will desire to thoroughly investigate someone before allowing that person to penetrate his boundary. This could cause others to feel isolated or walled out of a personal or professional relationship. He needs to be aware of his tendency to set up walls instead of boundaries. His rigid boundaries may cause him to lose the ability to influence through accountability.

Listeners may have the tendency to set boundaries that are excessively stringent at first and excessively pliable once the relationship has been established. He may be difficult to approach at the beginning of a personal or professional interaction. The Listener will desire to move slowly in all relationships. He may speak with uncertain or grey language that could frustrate those who are looking for a solid black or white answer or solution. While the initial interaction may be difficult, once the relationship is established he may struggle with having loose and undefined boundaries. His slow pace and questionable boundaries may cause him to lose the ability to influence through accountability.

Becoming aware of our own areas of struggle is the first step in leading ourselves well. Understanding the struggles that others face allows us to truly influence those around us. The process of setting boundaries begins with an awareness of our unhealthy tendencies. Next, we need tools to help us to become more effective leaders.

Mark Twain said, "Always do right. This will gratify some people and astonish the rest."

If only we could always "do right" as Twain suggests. The fact is that none of us are perfect. REAL Accountability is not an exact science. It takes practice and that comes with successes and failures. However, there are tools and processes that will help to make better decisions as we invest in others.

Boundaries guide us in our investments of time and energy with people as well as with our pursuits of success. Developing boundaries in the area of what and who we give ourselves to, is something only we can do.

The following tools are questions we may want to ask before we invest ourselves in the process of REAL accountability in a relationship or a course of action:

- Is what I want only appealing because it is self-serving?
- Do I want this or does someone else want it for me?
- Do I have what it takes to make this investment?
- Do I have the commitment to see it through?
- Will this benefit me in a meaningful way?
- Can I grow through this?
- Can I serve or help others by doing this?
- What must I avoid if I decide to go forward with this?
- Where is the danger zone?
- How will I know when I am close to going off course?

Possessing good boundaries shows we have respect for others and for ourselves. It shows we know our limits and will respect the limitations of others. What we say and what we do will define the boundaries we have or do not have.

Choosing to practice the behavior of setting strong and effective boundaries will allow us to execute REAL Accountability with incredible results.

Chapter Ten
Applying REAL Accountability

Accountability is just a word unless it is accompanied by action. This requires us to be intentional in the execution of these tools. In other words, REAL accountability is most effective when practiced on a regular basis. Practical application of the principles that we have discussed is essential to the success of any leader.

Here are some tips that will help us to apply real accountability in our everyday lives.

Relate Accountability: Tips

Remember when leading the Relate accountability type that he is best held accountable when convinced that he is accepted and valued as a person. He needs to know the individual holding him accountable is engaged and interested. When giving accountability to the Relate style we need to remember the following: He can receive accountability best when he feels respected.

Respect to a Relater is received through positive affirmation. This includes influencing through words, nonverbal expressions, and connection. The Relate accountability type will flourish with structure that is flexible and therefore will struggle in a rigid, stale work environment. It is important to realize that he may view accountability as conflict. Therefore setting clear expectations and defining goals is essential. This individual may over-personalize criticism. Therefore clarifying the reason for your criticism is important. The Relater can receive criticism that is grounded with his or her best interest in mind. Accountability given with verbal communication and validation is the key to successfully influencing the Relater.

If you are a Relater remember that accountability is not a personal attack. You must not base your self worth on feedback received from others. Being held accountable can be a positive and enriching experience. Choose to be open to constructive criticism and hard conversation.

EXECUTE ACCOUNTABILITY: TIPS

When giving accountability to the Execute style, we need to remember that she can best be held accountable when convinced that she is empowered to perform her job with authority. She needs to know the individual holding her accountable is confident in her ability to achieve the goal.

Respect to the Executer is given through empowerment. The execute accountability type will flourish with structure that is results driven. In other words, given the freedom to accomplish the task with minimal directions will equal validation for the Executer. Realize that accountability may be seen as a competitive challenge for the Executer. Once the goal or expectation has been given, she will work hard to achieve her task. This individual may have a tendency to dominate or run over others in her quest to accomplish her task. The Executer can best receive accountability with direct communication. Accountability that gives feedback at the end of a defined milestone or at the accomplishment of a goal is key to successfully influencing the Executer.

If you are an Execute type remember that people are important. Accountability is not a win or lose competition. You must guard against treating others as tools instead of individual people. Accountability can be used to strengthen relationships as well as to accomplish the task.

Analyze Accountability: Tips

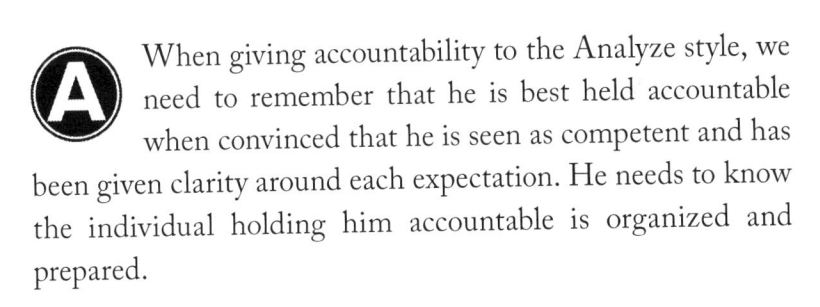

When giving accountability to the Analyze style, we need to remember that he is best held accountable when convinced that he is seen as competent and has been given clarity around each expectation. He needs to know the individual holding him accountable is organized and prepared.

Respect is given to the analyze type when he is presented with an organized plan. He sees a lack of organization and clarity as disrespectful. The Executor will flourish in a detailed structure with clear and defined expectations. Realize that accountability may be seen as rules to be followed. The Executor will work hard to follow the rules and processes that are given to him. In order to feel validated the Analyzer must receive feedback on a consistent basis. Accountability given with fairness for all, centering on the competencies at hand, is the key to successfully influencing the Analyzer.

If you are an Analyzer type remember that some things are more important than being technically correct. You must choose not to fact find when instead, listening and understanding is needed. Accountability is more than a process to ensure perfection; it is a way to connect with others.

Listen Accountability: Tips

When giving accountability to the Listen style, we need to remember that she is best held accountable when convinced that she is valued for her wisdom and insight. She needs to know that the individual holding her accountable is authentic and balanced.

Respect is given to the Listener by taking the time to authentically hear her. Because Listeners are generally introverted, it is important to slow down and invest in the relationship. The Listener will flourish when given deadlines for expectations and goals. The structure needs to be flexible yet provide appropriate boundaries for the task or project. Realize that accountability may be viewed by the Listener as too much structure. Therefore, give feedback on a personal one-on-one basis. Once the Listener is convinced that you are authentically invested, he will go to great lengths to meet your expectations.

Accountability given with humility and patience is the key to successfully influencing the Listener.

If you are the listen type remember that passivity breeds frustration. You must confront difficult issues in a timely manner. Accountability can be uncomfortable, yet it is a necessity that can lead to deep and powerful relationships.

Conclusion

The manner in which we live our lives speaks volumes about our commitment to practicing personal accountability. We persuade no one to follow us by saying one thing and doing another. REAL accountability is about more than just personal responsibility or maintaining a moral and ethical compass; this call to accountability is about personal growth and achieving one's maximum potential to influence. It is about committing to invest your life by reaching out to others. It is about choosing to practice the discipline of REAL accountability.... not with perfection but with consistency.

No doubt you have had opportunities to be a leader in some way during your life. Every day, all of us have the opportunity to choose how we are going to lead ourselves. Your success in life is not solely about reaching your destination, but about making the most of the opportunities along the journey.

At the end of your journey, you will not judge your life a success based on what you have done but on who you have influenced. So, the question at this point is: How are you influencing others?

Influencing through accountability requires the application of what we have learned thus far and more. However, to put things in perspective let's look at some ideas for practically applying the truths found in the previous chapters.

Understanding our individual accountability style is essential for personal accountability. We must first become aware of our own needs and desires before we can truly impact the lives of others. REAL accountability begins with the determination of our unique accountability style. Discovering if we are a Relater, Executer, Analyzer, or Listener is the first step.

This is where personal discipline becomes critical. Influencing others requires a person to control or manage himself well. It is no one else's responsibility, nor within another's ability, to control your thoughts, energy, focus, attitude, and actions. You are uniquely qualified to do this. You are responsible for your own behavior and ultimate accountability.

We are the only one who can choose how to live our individual life. People may force us into leadership, but no one can force us to lead or live with excellence. Taking our life to a new level of accountability, therefore, is up to us. Excellence is important because it is the distinguishing feature that sets something or someone above all that surrounds it. It exemplifies quality, whether it is in relation to a product or one's performance.

Conversely, one of the best ways we can put the quality of accountability in perspective is to consider the opposite of excellence—mediocrity. Mediocrity is all about being on the low end of average. It's just getting by. It's being happy with the status quo. It embodies the absence of dreams and goals. It is the apathy that slowly eats away at hope.

Accountability drives us to be more than we are or others think we can be. The question you and I answer each day is, "Will I pursue excellence in each area of my life?" This is what it takes to make an impact on those around us.

If we are committed to influencing through accountability, our communication and ability to connect must be taken to the next level. We must work on our message, our attitude and our motive. Choosing to become a student of how to interact with people of diverse personalities and accountability styles will serve both them and us. Consequently, we will reap the benefits of these relationships and be able to take them to a new level.

As one who wants to lead and influence others, you can take accountability to a new level through the discipline of crucial conversations. Healthy communication involves considering differing perspectives and working toward finding common ground. It is less about personal likes and dislikes and more about different approaches to accomplishing something or solving a problem. It is using diversity to inspire creativity. It is taking divergent thoughts and ideas and developing a consensus. It is taking the time to find out why there is disagreement and the merit of each perspective and bringing together the best from each. Influencing through REAL accountability does not come without having hard conversations. However, these crucial but necessary interactions allow us to create clarity that leads to higher productivity and performance.

Author and lecturer Denis Waitley once said, "The greatest communication skill is paying value to others." The person who leads others at a new level is the one who understands everything is not about him and that this has to be communicated to others by noting their contribution and value above his own. He understands others are looking for more than guidance or direction from those they follow. It's great to have a plan. It's good to have people with talent and ability to execute that plan. However it is encouragement and affirmation that supply the motivation for those we lead and love.

Well-thought-out boundaries will help a person stay true to herself and her values. Personal boundaries are an essential part of good decision-making skills. The result of healthy boundaries will be a clearer picture of who we are and what really matters to us in life. Boundaries also allow us to positively influence by giving and receiving accountability.

Finally, the science of EQ is a game changer for navigating successful relationships. Taking the time to invest in the process of developing our Self Awareness, Self Management, Social Awareness, and Relationship Management skills will yield immeasurable rewards on multiple levels. This may be the most powerful information about relationships that has been discovered to date. I hope that this small book and our humble offering of these principles will propel you to investigate the EQ world in a practical and applicable fashion.

As you are becoming aware, influencing through REAL accountability requires effort. Now that you have completed volume 2 of the EAGLE Leadership Series, we challenge you to continue to invest in your personal growth and in your relationships with others. As you choose to be accountable in your relationships with others you will begin to see its value more than ever. You will begin to reap the rewards of healthy relationships and you will see your influence with others increase.

My vision for this project is to provide you with the knowledge and tools to effectively influence others through accountability. This is no easy task. It takes commitment, discipline and hard work.

It is my desire that you will join me in the daily mission of speaking into the lives of others. Together we can **Make A Difference**!

R E A L

Works Cited

Badaracco, J. L. *Questions of Character: Illuminating the heart of leadership through literature.* (Boston: Harvard Business School Press 2006).

Covey, S. (n.d.), *Stephen Covey.* Retrieved November 11, 2011, from StephenCovey.com: https://www.stephencovey.com/7habits/7habits-habit4.php

Cloud, H. A., *Boundaries: When to Say Yes, How to Say No to Take Control of Your Life.* (Grand Rapids: Zondervan 2002).

Gerard Manley Hopkins, C. P. (2009). Gerard Manley Hopkins: The Major Works (Oxford World's Classics). In G. M. Hopkins, *Gerard Manley Hopkins: The Major Works (Oxford World's Classics).* Oxford University Press, USA; Reissue edition .

Grohol, J. M., *PsychCentral.* Retrieved February 1, 2011, from Psychcentral.com: http://psychcentral.com/lib/2009/fixing-cognitive-distortions/.

Kerry Patterson, J. G., *Crucial Conversations: Tools for talking when stakes are high .* (McGraw-Hill Companies, Inc. 2011).

Larry Little, *Make a Difference: The Challenge of Excellence, Volume 1 of the Eagle Leadership Series*. (IUniverse 2012).

Maxwell, J. C., *Everyone Communicates, Few Connect: What the most effective people do differently*. (Nashville: Thomas Nelson 2010).

Samuel, Mark. &. **Chiche, Sophie** *The Power of Personal Accountability: Achieve what matters to you*. (Katonah, NY: Xephor Press 2004).

The Hammer Principle. Concentrated Knowledge™ for the Busy Executive. www.summary.com. Vol. 27, No. 12 (2 parts), Part 2, December 2005. Order # 27-30.

Waitley, D. *Seeds of Greatness*. (New York: Gallery Books 2010).

Printed in the United States
By Bookmasters